GRAY MATTER

POETS OUT LOUD | Elisabeth Frost, *series editor*

SARA MICHAS-MARTIN **GRAY MATTER**

Fordham University Press | New York   2014

Library of Congress Control Number: 2013954287

Printed in the United States of America
16 15 14   5 4 3 2 1
First edition

For Andreas

CONTENTS

How much of a body is a spirit, and vice versa? Does the biology of our minds make for our behavior, become our destinies? Can we make choices not determined by the chemistries that make up our brains? What does this mean for free will and fate, and for faith itself? Is the spirit quantifiable?

Each era of scientific revolution—a reconceiving of our world as well as the terms in which science defines it—has had its own profound poetries, from Geoffrey Chaucer's *The Canterbury Tales* to William Carlos Williams's *The Desert Music and Other Poems*. Now Sara Michas-Martin's *Gray Matter* evokes our most immediate scientific revolution, the discovery of the interdependence of biology and environment—even if we don't yet understand to what extent each is altered by the other, and just what the effects may be. It is no accident that its title echoes that of George Oppen's post-nuclear masterpiece, *The Materials*. As Oppen presaged, material is altered by matter's will.

Gray Matter is indeed the manuscript's *matter:* gray in its infinite gradations; the material of the marks on the page written language makes; the hardwired biology of our brains as well as the matter of our thinking and sensing, our expectations for ambiguity; and how the best writing is obtained via precise utterance and image, as in the book's opening lines:

Hello internal assembly team.
I am un-singular today in this rash of faces.
I sense the careful in me trolling.

Is the sound of someone crying inside of us or outside of us? What is it in our wiring that (falsely) constructs continuity? What would it mean to let go into just that that overwhelms us? What *matter* makes our camp cabin-mate pull her eyelashes out, blissfully? At the heart of all of the questions in *Gray Matter* is the dance, the negotiation, between imagination and science, perception and thought.

The language in these poems juxtaposes the abstract precision of vocabularies around *thought* with viscerally precise descriptions of material events, tacking, with urgency, from surprise to surprise. "*Could these things be happy, in the way ice cream is happy?*" asks the prose poem "How Are You Feeling?" "There must be a moose somewhere in the yard. And a harpoon and a pint of oil," it continues. Undogmatic, the poems in *Gray Matter* still press upon us the precariousness with which selves and communities are constituted, and how errant, in the end, any notion of control may be in their construction. Wry, profound, these poems move like quicksilver.

This is a stunning, important collection of poetry: a book with a strong through-line that doesn't come close to feeling programmatic; nuanced and deftly balanced in its figures and forms, without ever calling attention to its intelligent use of each; steely and economical in its syntax, as we expect great poetry to be; and, in the end, multivalent and porous, giving the reader plenty of entrances and the room to arrive at varied readings each time through.

That these poems also plumb what is most fundamentally altered in our new world is pure boon.

Susan Wheeler
External Judge, 2012–13 Poets Out Loud Prize

ACKNOWLEDGMENTS

Grateful acknowledgment is made to the editors of the following journals in which forms of these poems originally appeared:

American Poetry Review: "Off Season," "Staff After Hours"
Anderbo: "What to Name This"
The Believer: "Cage"
Bird Dog: "Tryst"
Court Green: "Trichotillomania"
Denver Quarterly: "Crush," "Marriage"
DIAGRAM: "Spoil Song"
Elixir: "The Same and the Next"
FIELD: "The Empty Museum"
Forklift, Ohio: "In My Kid Bed, Sleeping, Shotguns Stored Below"
H_NG M_N: "In a Time of Transition"
Harvard Review: "Please Do Not Touch"
Hayden's Ferry Review: "Vision"
Hunger Mountain: "Illusion of One"
Iowa Review: "Return"
Podium: "Problems to Solve: Methods Invented"
Pool: "Desire," "For Better"
Prairie Schooner: "More Than One Way to Drown"
The Rumpus: "Cotard Syndrome"
Spoon River Poetry Review: "All Night I Felt My Teeth Loosening,"
    "Utility"
Squaw Valley Review: "Friendship South"
Third Coast: "Elegy"
Threepenny Review: "In Sleep the Brain Retrieves a Snake"
Word For/Word: "Café, Person Crying," "Gustation," "If I Think
    About It," "Audition"

"Return" was reprinted on *Poetry Daily*. "Cage" also appeared in *Best New Poets 2011*, edited by D. A. Powell. "Marriage" was reprinted on *Verse Daily* and later chosen as one of five "Verse Daily Favorite Poems of 2011." "Cotard Syndrome" was reprinted in *The Rumpus Original Poetry Anthology*, edited by Brian Spears (2012).

Thank you to the following programs, organizations, and people for providing generous support and invaluable community during the writing of this book: Stanford University's Wallace Stegner Program, Bread Loaf Writers' Conference, Squaw Valley Community of Writers, Napa Valley Writers' Conference, Hall Farm Center, Vermont Studio Center, University of Arizona Poetry Center, and the Dorothy Sargent Rosenberg Memorial Fund. Thank you to my friends, colleagues, and co-conspirators in the arts: Christina Ablaza, Gail Browne, Sommer Browning, Mary Beth Carolan, Robin Ekiss, Adam Johnson, Tom Kealey, Shara Lessley, Mary Popek, Rita Mea Reese, Alexandra Teague, Lysley Tenorio, and Malena Watrous.

For their insightful readings of this manuscript I am indebted to Kirsten Anderson, Patrick Donnelly, Keith Ekiss, Ken Fields, Maria Hummel, Ann Keniston, Mike McGriff, Hilton Obenzinger, Bruce Snider, Kristen Tracy, and Nance Van Winckel. Thank you, Susan Wheeler, for choosing the manuscript, and Fordham University Press for making it a book. Elisabeth Frost, thank you for being the most thoughtful editor imaginable.

For their kindness and enduring mentorship, I owe a debt of gratitude to Eavan Boland, Simone Di Piero, Larry Goldstein, Tony Hoagland, Jane Miller, the late Steve Orlen, Boyer Rickel, Frances Sjoberg, Ellen Bryant Voigt, Tobias Wolff, and Dean Young. I am grateful for my family, the Koopses, Martins, and Michases, and I am indebted especially to Joanne Martin Braun, who first showed me there was an inner and outer world worth exploring. And to my mother, Gail, who taught me it was okay to color outside the lines. Andreas, without your unwavering support and love this book would not be.

There are continual gaps in our seemingly solid world.

—Chögyam Trungpa, *The Myth of Freedom*

I wake and I'm one person, and when I go to sleep I know for certain I'm someone else.

—Bob Dylan, *Newsweek*

GRAY MATTER

Illusion of One

Hello internal assembly team.

I am un-singular today in this rash of faces.

I sense the careful in me trolling.

An itch welling at the crown.

My shadow: *no.   yes.   fast.   approximate.*

Operations make up your mind.

I'm a looped syllable.

A white point diving and rising all over the map.

One self looks out over another

and perceives a *you.*

In Sleep the Brain Retrieves a Snake

The mind rallies its fragments:
my sister
        a Safeway stock boy
my car an empty television box.
        And recently
the return of the snake

sliding through my house, a lean-to
made of cambio receipts

and not in Arizona but in Maine
on a beach in the off season.

        Of course I know
this snake, the scene
from which it was extracted.

The girl from San Francisco
with the bracelets and cigarettes

passes a bag of pineapple
        slick and leaking
from her hammock to mine.

She was waiting for the boy in India.
I was waiting
for a balloon version of myself

to part a seam in the sky.

The thump
falling through what passed for a roof
            was the snake.
It coiled and flapped on the cement slab
its skin synthetic green.

I reached to touch it
so cool   so heavy
            that slippery stand-in

for some category of dark.

Please Do Not Touch

When I touch my husband sometimes
I'm stroking my own arm. I arrange
his curls as if they're sticking up
on my own head. The knobs on his hips
are open territory for my thumbs
as are the rough patches on his elbows
he had me pinch once with pliers
to prove we have no nerve endings there.
Sometimes his touch can whet
every cell in me as the hands
on the clock fan out and briefly form an L
for *license, liaise*, for *lost* and *ludicrous*,
for light passing through
the slats of the backyard fence I climb
to touch the weight of the word love.
Not the love a mile underground
on a train that slows into the station
like a sore arm bending, but the kind
boarded on a ship and sailed hard
into the storm we've made of ourselves.
I was too young once to touch my mouth
to a boy's mouth, to attempt a range of pressures
before deciding kissing someone was like kissing
the inside of a warm tomato. *Honey,*
don't touch repeated in the kitchen
and in the museum where the school takes me
to learn about native peoples. I'm not allowed
to touch the lady stirring the pot
in the lifelike diorama. I do not touch
the birch wood bowls or polished arrowheads,

not even the orange and brown
plastic leaves. But I'm touching
the inside of my clothes *Mrs. Bean*,
and my teeth touch the teeth next to them
and my earring, a hoop my sister
jammed through my ear, that's
touching and my eyelashes when I blink
and my lips if I stop talking. Most of us
pass through the grip of the cervix
and recollect nothing. Babies will die
of touch starvation. Orphans reach
half a child's normal height.
I was too young once
for any body of water to feel
too cold for swimming. Too young
to feel my capillaries seal closed,
to keep my towel from dragging
through poison ivy, to know cutting an X
in the first blister with my fingernail
would do nothing but spread the rash
further up my legs. I was too young
to know the oil on my fingers
would damage the monarch's wing,
too young to know the dog's gluey eye
was not a marble to play with.

Elegy

Lake Michigan is growing smaller. Each time I go home more of the beach
shows its ratty, pocked face. I dream the Greeks are responsible, I see them—
climbing the old peeling stairs. Each man carries a piece of lake up past

the gold shops, steaming bakeries, rows of fish and unpronounceable cheese.
Back home the neighbors struggle to get their boats in the water. My father
cuts open his toe swimming. When a new sandbar appears, it's flagged

and named for its uncommon shape. Working faster and all the time now, the men
are moving Lake Michigan. In a room I don't remember, although
the floor is familiar, I've surrendered to infection. Fever spreads

under my skin, concentrates at the tonsils. All the time the men marching—
what looks like thick glass tucked under their arms. The hostel owner
places olives on his tongue one at a time. His wife prays near the cash box.

When the doctor comes he kneels by the mattress I've made hot with fear,
a silk curtain floats between his shoulders. He says *go home. Your throat is closing.*
It's not the lonely descent over Detroit that's stale and grim, it's what happens

to the northern woods. Everyone sleeping when I get there. The flag waves
on the sandbar and Lake Michigan is gone. There are no sounds
in the canyon. No sounds pass through the fields of bleached elk bones.

If I Think About It

The owl strains to cough a pellet forward
I wait at the table   gloved   with tweezers
to untangle a complete set of bones   to rebuild
a swallowed vole   you might say the body
is awash with industry   the mind
bears down to evolve   to weed through
the intake   whole sequences
made skinny   tapered to a glimpse
a friend crossed out misspelled words
with a ruler   I shoved her cat   more than once
down the chute   but her name
eludes me   because each night
I am a coast   reconfigured by a storm
moving this fast   impossible to follow
anything down to its unhammered root
back up from the filmstrip   see the levers
and blue canals   take on abstract qualities
say the edge   is more casually defined
you'll feel uplifted   the lesson
stays clinical   but the word *artery*
can be a red flower I shape with my voice
or the name of a country   I invent
just so I can leave it.

Female Dorm, Barcelona

Nineteen people sleep
in this room, this onion cave.
Nineteen whistles
dragging oxygen. Nineteen
funnels of up-and-down light
while our stories cross
on the other side. Passports
disappear up stranger's sleeves
or slip into subway grates
where insects devour
our given names. With great effort
we move behind the interpreter.
We follow directions
to keep our costumes plain.
The moon controls
the migration of our eggs
but we don't understand how.

The Empty Museum

Plumbed from a cadaver, the brain
inside a jar is a cloud of coils
and magnified, the way a fish
when it swims to the corner of a tank
looks inflated; a government
that's lost its country, an eyeball loose
trolling the dungeons of the sea.
Some people love the color pink
so much they wear pink sweaters
and purchase pink cars
and juice them up and down
the highway. The brain is the color
of the road, of the Midwest gloom
that hangs in the spindle left of trees
past winter. I carry that hue inside me
like clay-scented air. It's a twisted tether
and sometimes inside my dream
as the day heats up around me
it's a rustic sort of place
I can't back away from. The guide
says the self is elastic, it fogs over, twins.
We engineer a filter and backload a story.
I ask to touch the brain, maybe hold it
and when I do, its weight tests
the give of both hands. I think of bowling
and watermelons floating in a pool, an infant
translating the blast of shadows
that enter a room. I forget
and I remember. I can tap a memory
of a boy in his yard carving a moat

around an underground animal
making noise with its teeth.
I think of summer still
as an entrance to the palace
where the sun actually lives.
I bused north growing up
to a green-blue place
where a herd of us smuggled
an orange life preserver through the woods
without getting tagged. There was a girl
who would die in college. I see her
on the dock in a towel like a cape,
hair dripping with lake water.
When she passed
songs we learned with God in the chorus
stopped living in her brain.
A person travels with a net
collecting for the factory. A person
passes a window and feeds on the view.
Under a large and unfamiliar hat
a person lifts her chin at the mirror
tilts her face to the side, then looks away
and back again, her whole life
the same question: I'm not sure
if this is *me*. I shake the brain
wanting a file to slip, a him or
a her knitted in tissue, odd muzzle
under fixative. If this pile—
folded, inscrutable—were alive
I picture a table cluttered with jewelry,
the light jumping all over it.

How Are You Feeling?

What do you mean? *I mean, what would you pick to fill the cloud adrift in your abdomen?* Ferns from the backcountry. Or magenta. *Could these things be happy, in the way ice cream is happy?* There must be a moose somewhere in the yard. And a harpoon and a pint of oil. *Will you be staying outside the building?* Will you maintain that social smile? *Emotional changes are defined by myriad changes in the body's chemical profile.* When I shake a hand, I want to convey I'm hungry, but have my own supplies. *I thought you wanted to graduate?* I have devotion. *Tell me what I'm really hearing.* It's about to storm. But I stay in the water, my feet unprotected from the rocks. All the children are rounded up. I watch the families limp away. I'm thinking, I'm screwed. Without a ride, I'm really screwed. *In these circumstances the reflex would belong to the organism but not necessarily "you."* Does my thin hair make you nervous? *The "after" process to which I am referring is not beyond the brain.* I want more conscious control of my organs. Confirmation they're working properly. *Please sit down.* I want my brain to be less domestic. *Proto-self.* To stop cutting out. *Self-same.* To pin down the main idea. To get away with lying, to switch off its theatre, have nothing to report.

Cage

On one side of the world two men argue
over the placement of sticks as they lay a fire

in the woods near the festival. The fire
attracts many people who shake to the sound

of hands slapping drums. On the other side
kids unpack their water guns, their little sacks of flour

and build stupas out of sand in the river.
I sit in the hard dirt looking all around

and try to be glad for one thing. But watch
a seated crowd from a distance

notice.how many people touch their faces, or wave
their arms, as if to form one animal stuck

on its back. Once a year it's tradition to purchase
a white bird in a wire cage, only to walk a few feet

and release it. I'd be less restless
if I could, periodically, let one thing go—

a spider inside a suitcase, the voice
of someone I despise. I could smile truthfully

across a fire at someone with whom I may
never speak. If you and I ever meet, dear stranger

on a bumpy train, in a car where we are forced
to face each other and become anxious

enough to talk, let's talk frankly
and about uncommon things.

All Night I Felt My Teeth Loosening

Bangkok, 1999

Quiet waits in the Shrine
at Turtle Mount   I buy cheese and a stick
from the monks   extend my arm
                    to the creatures
            dividing the blackness of the pond

at home we spear marshmallows
try and scare each other
                    in the dark

every male here ordained
I watch
            the young novice bow   make offerings
to his teacher

even this hot the city swells
            a coherence of bees   aimlessness
                    absorbed easily   then appetite
then aimlessness

across the ocean
they evict mountain lions from Madera Canyon
            two teenagers   shoot up their school

my dentist says
                    losing teeth
is a woman's dream   common
            and associated with vanity

the brain sees film canisters

floating in the pond   lychee pits   bottles

       arrives at snow   the lost feeling of wool

what it's like to sit

    in a car frosted over.

Return

I walk to make certain I was ever there.
To find the car I once discovered

buried in the pines   as if it were left
for the mushrooms to affix   for crows

to pull batting from its seats.   Small
when I see it   body rubbed free of paint

roof caved   like a chocolate egg   left in the rain
and the myths are gone   the witch

I thought placed it here   the silver horses
that drag cars off many roads.

Now I imagine   before trees filled in
someone drove   just this far   and parked.

Up here   the water
driving against the northern shore

just one layer of silence
spread thin inside another.

More Than One Way to Drown

Again   last night
pinning me down   what I now call
the phantom.   She was there

my mother   *wake up* she said
hurry.   I couldn't move my arms or legs
my mouth and eyes

stayed sealed.   They say   *Isolated*
Sleep Paralysis.   They say   *medicine*
medicine.   Years ago   seeing my mother

by the sink   I darted across the field
a trout pulsing in each hand.   *Look*
what I caught   what I pulled

from the water.   But the misstep
the conjured image   a child curled
on the bottom of a well pond.   I see

through tempered glass my own
stone extremities.   As if I've fallen
beyond sleep.   My body's unbound

intact   a rabbit frozen
in the wood pile   or one of the fish
dropped in the grass.   My mother

on instinct   restored my breath.
But the dog was changed.
And the child?   Trout swirl up

from the brush pile.   They puff their gills
and flash their rainbow skin.
They say   there are no hands on me

no shadows near the bed.   She says
it's the pond inside   the last drops
thrashing their way out.

To Know It Again

The mind has some idea
of what to do
because it's always been invested
in the enterprise of seeing,
keeping track
of how something feels
and how it operates and if
it's been here before, certain
about the death of many cells
or the time in line at the bank
you hugged the wrong mother.
It's a notable occasion
to get the thug dancing,
to ride a green light
finding north and think
I'll try this once more
despite everyday distortions
including the fish too large
for the back seat or the tone
you misread for arrogant.
Around the head
stirs a haze of gases
and you recall a similar time
you climbed a fallen tree
the connection
still very alive, also your way
of being yourself to yourself.
Continuity, that myth.

Olfaction

Heat breaks against the city   rats canvass garbage
before the sun livens the stench   overtaking steam
from the rusted waffle cart   the neighbor's chain-smoke
wafting through the a/c   where I linger
attempting to daydream the temperature
of Lake Superior   trout swimming vertically
adrift from natal streams
who smell for trace particles   to follow home   to breed
some shared design of early human   before our creature
staggered out of the ocean   breathing on half-formed lungs
testing new measures of gravity   brain sprouting
around the olfactory bulb   it's impossible
to name directly   a scent that opens on you
like a fire alarm   carrot yanked clear out of the ground
or the whisper you inhale   from a few rooms over
to confirm nothing is burning   no poisonous vapor
not your nerves in bloom   like years ago   the swim meets
how I shook on the starting block   the smell of chlorine
a kind of scar   on the limbic target   which lives
where memory lives   and why I recall
in the after burn of matches   a lover   mid-day
lighting a candle   the window closed on a mower
the tone at his neck   something like   bleach and grass
which calmed me   the way gas fumes can
coasting into a station   those lost miles
en route to upper Michigan   where the sky
claims enormous real estate   and I drive into it
on the wind   barely the mention of cattle.

In My Kid Bed, Sleeping, Shotguns Stored Below

Each night the head-first of me hoisted in the maelstrom. I see
the clotted system, hear all of it, a chorus of clasping iron. Children lowered
into swimming holes with cranes. Villages galvanized and feasting. I carry

a license to conceal my stereo. Everything I bend or handle is low-voice,
half-void and peeling around the collar. A man cradles his inherited
toxin. Large tears in his foul weather gear. Cars hang from power lines.

People trapped inside raise fingers to the tigers prowling. The whole populace
swings on tethers above a blue fire that dilates, reclines. I'm not familiar
with the grand accident. I pause to fall down repeatedly. The swamp

is bruised with runoff, backwash, overflow. *Look around you, say something
to anybody.* One daisy among smashed down fruit. A caucus stirs
in the outer banks, shallow words, gravel flying.

Vision

When any matter
is before me
I absorb the information of its outline.

Translated signals
pulse through seven layers
of alternating cells
to the back of my head

where I compose an inverse image
while deciding
what to think about it.

*

Reading her expression
could be as hard as assembling a 10-speed bicycle
that arrives in a hundred pieces
and is the only way to the store.

*

A streetcar rumbles through the frame
full of spaced-out passengers staring into phone wires
that surge invisibly with things
chosen to be said out of view.

*

From the sky
order imposed in perfectly measured plots.

The untouched spans in between
could persuade a person
the earth is winning.

*

The woman in P-Town, how does she keep the silver bird
from leaving her shoulder?

*

The answer depends
on what it's like now
to stand before a Great Lake.
Am I weightless in this pause
or weighted by the depth of field
methodically folding in on itself?

*

Out of the land, Olmsted crafted experience
positioning switchbacks and steep overlooks
he wanted people to work for.

*

The street vendor craves often
an aerial view.

*

The sun isn't really shining until someone sees that it is.
There are more than enough windows to look through.

*

When people are lost
they begin traveling in circles.
That's what German scientists
have confirmed we're programmed to do.

They can't say why
though have ruled out
as a possible cause
our uneven legs.

Friendship South

We boxed horns, me and her.
            We weren't even
mechanically nice.

She was the leaner and I the seeker
and the roles expired.

Time I knew would not come back
                  or that feeling
when we rummaged like raccoons
for a clip of the funny.

            I tried clearing the flue.
I was the neck of the chimney
being plunged. Also the one
wielding the instrument.

This house, I thought,
            it's coming down,
and it was.

But those years, all of them
and without turbulence
            squeezed from the rafters.

            The hole in the air
might have swallowed me
            had I not turned away.

What to Name This

Chronic things like wonder
and fog came up fugitive around me.

Your experience
was it so different?

Chevron, Indian River Medicine, Murdock's, Stop—
we stole many signs

and flower baskets and orange cones and the Dairy Queen graphic.

We should have known better than to laugh.
We claimed our gravity
and the chance to cry openly around a guitar. Or was it

like mistaking the sound of wind
for waves at high altitudes. I'm not sure.

The lake today, clear to the bottom.
Giant carp pass under the boat
like apparitions
like memories of carp.

The Same and the Next

My friends find a torn photograph off the highway
and another and pieces in the woods.
They assemble like detectives at the picnic table,
tell me my ponytail is shaped like the girl's
who holds something green in the air, inside a glass.
There's a scene by a lake I might recognize. Two figures
darkened by the glow of a sun going down.
The lighting strange in others.
Beer bottles litter a floor, a white tulip
unlaced on a chair. How many dogs
are buried in my neighborhood?
Yards of hair loosening while I sleep, bone
breaking down and what grows there.

Spoil Song

The man poses in the trees as a lion with a crooked tail.

He looks on the two girls with animal regret, if only he could play,

if they might want him. The upturned willow was commissioned

by the river. All afternoon he watches. The girls

leap from the willow. They hang their suits in the branches. Girls, girls

the world tells him. Girls should not sleep in the woods.

Their dinner, their fire, he watches. Pretend bear. Pretend gun.

In the air, a coal perfume. They wake twice—in the trash, raccoons.

Inside the tent they might want him. Not the raccoons,

not the bear. Girls should not sleep. Never animals

that bother you. One girl pulls at the other's hair to wake her.

Again, the raccoons.   A deer then.   The lake.   No.   What

teaches them not to sleep. The man crouched over them.

Without light what teaches them. Soured air. Car keys.

He mentions the gun, crouched over them. Bear sighting,

there is a bear. They might want him with no light. Black bears

don't bother you. What teaches one to play along. *Over there.*

Stand guard. Thank god you'll help us. A little actress

in a fake play. What teaches her what to say. What teaches her

to quiet the other. To unlock the car. Thank him. To drive away.

Desire

Catalyst and camouflage.
Enemy of indifference.
Drool trigger. Heat
before the burn, before
the blister. Sonorous fog
with invisible hooks.
Suggestive of
but not limited to
the state of being thirsty.
Seduced potentially
and fueled by the unknown
and/or the weight of never
not being thirsty.
What leaks the animal out.
What installs the internal grip.
Having or able to thaw,
as in *his handsome*
meant her sinking.
To bruise for. To become
easily bruised by. Impulse
to accelerate, as in *a horse*
speeds the barn, a baby
speeds the mother, as in *I*
speed the door that opens
to something better.
Furred and sticky noun

not always
in an orange-red coat—
I can't see you
blow into the noise
of the street, or myself
either, out of breath
crashing after you.

Trichotillomania

Little bald girl, we call you
and *hatchet-lady kin, dragon mane*
and *maniacal.* Because
of your ugly-making habit
we don't share our lip gloss.
We don't like your strange
brooding weather, or your face
without eyelashes because
you lie on your bunk, eyes
glazed with pleasure
and yank them all out.
We watch you, the way
you mope around
in your stained yellow flip-flops
thirsty for that pinch of hurt.
Does the urge come like a fever,
like a bird desperate to land
before you duck behind our cabin
or steal into a bathroom stall
to tear at the root
until your mouth waters?

Staff After Hours

They smell delicious plotting
      through the dark   not seeing themselves
            flooded or creaturely
      their spruced kissers
expedient and all together
      his breath dares her flutter awake
            while she dares his nerve and hers
      and those stirring the watch fire
naked in the water
      someone gropes for the deer mount
            its goofy snarl and patchwork hide
      a ruse underway   laughter in the pantry
the deer lifted into someone's sleep
      antlers askew   the watchers in hysterics
            rumor of a taxidermist gone blind.

Crush

I stared at it when I was hungry. I showed it to too many friends. I took it to bed with me and it was there waiting when I woke up. I tugged on its hair. I backed over it by accident with the car. It was stale. It was juicy. It was stale. It was looming. I wore away the corners with my active thumb. I backed over it with the car. And I backed over it again.

Audition

Halyards in the bay   steady the indoor voice of the water

the undertow mumbles its silhouette   an exhale

elevated to a sigh   the full amplitude of motion   any object

produces sound   when it vibrates in matter

particles collide   with particles in front of them

which collide   with particles ahead

until you hear water   hiss in the metal sink

pipes clacking elbows   the suck on the drain

over the whistle outside   echo of high heels

pigeon warble   trucks wincing through gears

hammer   anvil   stirrup

noise plays past the ear   marries us to time

its tricks with speed   and one-way argument

sitting quiet   the reward of nothing   then

letting a song decide   which mood to sink

what other faculties live as vacant   as crammed

as spotted as this?

Gustation

I wanted to know your country   I let you order

the terrible green egg   fluid aged two weeks

in the heat   then passed ceremoniously

to slurp through the homemade aperture

the aftertaste cast wide   sulfuric and murky

all that expires in the deep end of the farm

my most flexible cavity   stretched with bird

bird cycling the vein   already

bird-powered wrist   in my fabric

a little bird soul   a shell.

Tryst

The sheriff wants to investigate brains for a case
and I wear the keys to the gallery on my silver belt.

It works that I hold his brain for collateral. It's knotted
and less greasy than it looks. There's a crab

below the sheen, it raises a claw. I listen to the pathways
whistling, the bulked-out sensory line, the faint sound

of a suffering dog. The organ cools my hand
though flares in the busy places. I watch a thought

climb out of the river and perform on the banks.
The sheriff's shoes make egg shapes in the sand

as he glides between tanks tracing scrolls
through the formalin. He smiles a ripe smile

when he joins me at the counter, no hat.
I jab the turkey with a pencil when I think it's done.

If good at reading code he'll know I'm oiled and under-
sparked, a moth hovering a candle. Below trap doors

the water runs clear, the planet rides the current
blindly. Parts of myself duck behind tissues

when he uncaps my cranium. His gates swing open
and gloveless, the mass could burn. We scan

each other's classifieds. We fumble with the hurts—
my pawed-over memory, his shaken-down heart.

We wade through kelp groped wholly from our shells.

In a Time of Transition

The yellow trees on shore I try not to see
as any kind of explosion. The driver is faceless.

He has not been supplied a wheel. For now
I'm blank and unmoved by the sights.

Fish dart rapidly inside me.
An ache is slow to surface. I tell him

the bubble had already formed teeth. It's clear
he loads this news remotely.

I close one eye to let the water come out.
I hold open the other to take the water in.

I want to honor the flood, I do.
Our plan to make many plans

is the small child clutching the towline
at the back of the boat. Already we have forgotten.

The child lets go and is left there.

Since He Asked

They saddle me with flatware,
I let the plants die
                    on purpose.

A music stand does not belong in a field.

          Materials arrive
in oversized boxes;
                    I should want this
                    and a white dress.

The temperature reads: *time to go*
          time to go.

I want Asia,
                    everything
(and him there too).

Water recovers muscle from wind,
this is true
for me also.

Marriage

One side at a time scientists paralyze the brain
then ask the other side questions. You told me
conflict was contagious. Eating eggs raw
I feel poisoned a little and on the highway
that stain is not from a deer. I was half asleep so
I missed what you said. Your hands on my
buttons. Me twisting your wheels. How often
does paint fly out of a truck? Bump the cortex
you'll hysterically laugh. Ever heard of a deer
with pink or green blood? Left half says
spinnaker. Right half: *I miss you, go fish.*
They hope to close the gap between unsure
and hailing. What if all day your job
was to retrieve ruined animals? When you're funny
I picture my left-glow, my inhibited amygdala.
Together we make an imperfect riot.
I mean, it's questionable either of our cities is real.

Imperfectly Divided

If questioned about our earthly floor
I answer, the mountain, or anything
made solid under where
I am standing.
If I can learn to keep still
I will grow a horn, hard as rock
and filled with gray matter
that becomes a hook for keys
to the front doors of every place
I have ever slept
which proves the sliding definition
of mountains or that keys
are like sequins
stitched into a dress
I can't wear anymore.
New leaves are made
with the same air and time
that form the mountain inside me
where the squawk is captive
until a crow dizzies out from the pack
and flies high enough
to become a star
that fades from the cornea
like one word
omitted from a sentence
preventing the meaning to hold.

Capgrass Syndrome

When the mind woke up, it flitted back and forth,
alerting the eyes. It understood patterns and shades
to mean a barren room and door. Very quickly it found
it could direct the body to sit up. It knew how
to vocalize answers when questions were asked
and the words seemed correct, people nodded, looked pleased.
The mind felt relief learning it had not been harmed
by the force of a great collision. It sensed it had
gone through the wash and come out remade
into something larger, more pliable. It recognized
the face that belonged to it. Flashes of a past
summarized his person. He knew who he was.
He named with ease the people he cared for.
Right away he knew that dented gold ring. His wife.
Her very red sweater. Her scent that echoed
the scent of new leaves. But he looked at her and he
looked at her and was sure she had been replaced.
The team explained the severed link and the line
that would not grow back. Which meant
loving the impostor was essential, was second life.

For Better

On your way to him   passing lanes of garlic
orchards spooling fruit   you are anyone
on the road.   You are anxious.   You are okay
in your laced shoes.   You search the radio's heart junk
for a voice that makes you listen.   Who are you
to the cow?   Miraculous cow like a coin in the grass.
Who are you to the crows who scan the air above?
You are tired.   You are hungry.   You are hungry
because you are anyone   sliding like a hollow bead
between two points.   You are your mother
who floods her liver   your father
who sucks the sweet out of cigarettes.
Their distance a sentence you read to the end   catch
and read again.   You're unsteady at weddings
of friends.   Identical vows   the same: *love is*
patient   love is kind . . . we are not
one glass   but share the same water . . .   Why not
Jack   you iron t-shirts   but are moved
by the bank commercial.   Jill   you're stormy.
You lose all my stuff   but my home is where you are
and you've never locked the door.

Problems to Solve: Methods Invented

from David E. Brown's *Human Universals*

Even the casual citizen knows the self
as subject and object, and speaks
her personal name. You have ways
of backward seeing, a camera,
mental maps and also
sidewalks, meal times, emerging
predictions. In-groups distinguished
from out-groups, there's gift-giving
and grieving, tool-making and
sweets preferred. Hairstyles. Turn-
taking. Folklore. Return
these items (grammar
hygienic care) to be refunded
completely. Flightless, in-range,
thumb-sucking—you've heard music
related in part to religious activity
and at some point have been
tattled on, translated,
classified by color, condition
and inner state. You wish to preserve
special speech for special occasions
and the vigilant safety
of someone. For five to ten hours
sleep occurs, which you enter
the way a canoe slides into water,
your breath the oar
turning you through.

Synaptic Sprawl

Please fill in box five
with your full please
fill in box five with box
five with your full box
please fill in box five
with your full given name.

Cotard Syndrome

Jeanie was well oriented for time, place and person . . .
as for being dead or alive, she was all at sea.
                    —Paul Broks, neuropsychologist

She sits in her usual chair,
her lips dry as dust.
          She's aware of her tongue
limp between her teeth.

She swallows water,
feels it slosh inside her chest.
Her organs, she says, sag out of place,
the rest of her
                    charting the ghost feed.

In time
her mouth will close into a scar.
She won't believe she has a face
to speak out of.

She senses death waiting: a driver
with a sign at the airport.

She is inside the terminal
somewhere counting backwards.

Café, Person Crying

The spirit unbundled like that

no place
proper to land

eye to eye   out of reach
the meanwhile

imprecise
the shared quality
of accents

a need to level
continuously   a script

burn spots   standing quickly
after not standing

hard to judge
for instance
corners on most people

from the margins
guesswork

some things
born without aid
or antonym

it's common in fading to ignore
a sigh let go

a short descent
radial sob

here   in this room together

innumerable the ways
we are not.

Utility

The body
beyond vehicle or desire
a mixed country of cells   one broad muscle moving

nude figure model
intent on holding a pose

artist behind newsprint
drafting the wrist and jawbone

the darks   the lights

soft nerve machine
that visits the doctor
when a part is down

nurse who travels the patient's chest
listening for the stutter.

Off Season

With nothing to hook on
the wind makes us sore with nothing
to hook on the leaves blow down
the pasture encased in snow
the fox skulks like a stain
its plume and casual lope
though it's us who parade
our summer fluency
which doesn't matter
in the see-through forest
its exposed cog and wheel
make us sore for dimension
washed out under the overcast
the lake water static and the dinner bell
frozen with the caretaker's venison
in the lodge we grow restless
around a picnic table moved inside
wood softened from the elements
we leave a knife in the middle
with nothing to hook on
inscribe our names as if
they were not generic: *we were*

    here   *we were*

        here.

"The Empty Museum" was written after an incognito visit to an anatomy lab, and inspired by an essay by Paul Broks titled "Soul in a Bucket."

Some of the italicized text in "How Are You Feeling" is taken from Antonio Damasio's book, *The Feeling of What Happens: Body and Emotion in the Making of Consciousness* (New York: Harcourt Brace, 1999).

Isolated Sleep Paralysis is a phenomenon that occurs when a person wakes up yet remains in a partial dream state and temporarily is unable to move voluntary muscle groups.

Frederick Olmsted, landscape architect most famous for co-designing New York's Central Park, advocated for the rights of all people to have access to the natural world, given nature's positive effects on human perception.

The egg in "Gustation" refers to a Vietnamese street food called *balut* (hột vịt linộn), a partially developed duck egg believed to be an aphrodisiac.

"Marriage" was inspired by the *Wada test*, a medical procedure that puts one cerebral hemisphere to sleep in order to test language and memory function in the other and is performed while the patient is fully conscious. The poem also draws from a long-standing marital debate.

Following a stroke, drug overdose, or accident causing damage to the brain, *Capgras syndrome* involves a disconnect between a person's ability to recognize something or someone and assign emotional significance. The primary delusion is that a close relative or spouse has been replaced by an impostor, an exact double, despite familiarity in appearance and behavior.

The *Diagnostic and Statistical Manual of Mental Disorders (DSM) IV* describes *Trichotillomania* as an impulse-control disorder characterized by the persistent and excessive pulling of one's own hair.

"Problems to Solve: Methods Invented" uses language from Donald E. Brown's anthropological text *Human Universals* (New York: McGraw-Hill, 1991).

Cotard syndrome is a psychiatric condition often associated with depression, in which a person may, incrementally, begin to have nihilistic delusions of losing parts of the body until the afflicted believes that he or she does not exist.

*

The texts named below were of particular influence, and I wish to thank the authors for making their ideas and research accessible.

Diane Ackerman, *An Alchemy of Mind* (New York: Scribner, 2004); Paul Broks, *Into the Silent Land: Travels in Neuropsychology* (New York: Atlantic Monthly Press, 2003); Antonio Damasio, *Self Comes to Mind: Constructing the Conscious Brain* (New York: Pantheon, 2010) and *The Feeling of What Happens: Body and Emotion in the Making of Consciousness* (New York: Harcourt Brace, 1999); Joseph LeDoux, *Synaptic Self: How Our Brains Become Who We Are* (New York: Penguin, 2003); V. S. Ramachandran, *A Brief Tour of Human Consciousness: From Impostor Poodles to Purple Numbers* (New York: Pi Press, 2004); V. S. Ramachandran and Sandra Blakeslee, *Phantoms in the Brain: Probing the Mysteries of the Human Brain* (New York: William Morrow, 1998); Oliver Sacks, *Musicophilia: Tales of Music and the Brain* (New York: Vintage, 2008); Rebecca Skloot, *The Immortal Life of Henrietta Lacks* (New York: Crown, 2010); and Chögyam Trungpa, *The Myth of Freedom and the Way of Meditation* (Berkeley: Shambhala Publications, 1976)

POETS OUT LOUD | Prize Winners

Sara Michas-Martin
Gray Matter

Peter Streckfus
Errings | EDITOR'S PRIZE

Amy Sara Carroll
Fannie + Freddie: The Sentimentality of Post–9/11
Pornography

Nicolas Hundley
The Revolver in the Hive | EDITOR'S PRIZE

Julie Choffel
The Hello Delay

Michelle Naka Pierce
Continuous Frieze Bordering Red | EDITOR'S PRIZE

Leslie C. Chang
Things That No Longer Delight Me

Amy Catanzano
Multiversal

Darcie Dennigan
Corinna A-Maying the Apocalypse

Karin Gottshall
Crocus

Jean Gallagher
This Minute

Lee Robinson
Hearsay

Janet Kaplan
The Glazier's Country

Robert Thomas
Door to Door

Julie Sheehan
Thaw

Jennifer Clarvoe
Invisible Tender